North Wa

Landscapes

Photographs Simon Kirwan

Text Hilary Ellis

MYRIAD
LONDON

North Snowdonia

The dominating Snowdon range is at the heart of north Snowdonia – a spectacular backdrop to the coastal scenery of all north-west Wales. Over half a million visitors each year come to climb the highest of Snowdonia's rugged ridges and summits, and to enjoy the scenery around the many beautiful lakes and valleys. Sailors travelling on ships from Ireland in the dark ages referred to the snow-covered peaks here as Snowy Hills (or Snaudune in Gaelic) and Snowdonia's main peaks were known as Yr Eryri, "the abode of the Eagles". The region is now a national park but scars of the slate industry can still be seen among the mountain crags.

Nant Ffrancon Pass *(above)*

The Afon Ogwen flows through the Nant Ffrancon Pass in this beautiful springtime scene. Travelling north on the A5, the rounded mounds of Foel Goch and Mynnydd Perfedd to the left overlook the lush green valley. Once a lake carved by glaciers would have been found here, but it has long gone. Now the flat meadowland is a peaceful haven among the formidable peaks of the surrounding mountains.

Nantgwynant Pass *(above)*

This beautiful wintry photograph overlooks the peaceful Nantgwynant valley from a viewpoint on the A498 to Beddgelert. Beneath the towering peaks of the Snowdon horseshoe, the pipeline carrying water from Llyn Llydaw can be seen clearly on the mountainside. Built in 1905, the Cwm Dyli hydroelectric power station in one of the oldest running in the UK today, with a single generator producing electricity for the National Grid.

Crib Goch & Snowdon *(left)*

The summit of Snowdon, known as Yr Wyddfa, is the highest point in Wales at 3,560ft (1,085m). Three popular hikes ascend to its grand summit. The Llanberis Track is the easiest route but alternatives include the Pyg Track and the Miner's Track. These early morning scenes are taken from the Miner's Track, once used by men who worked in copper mines high in the mountains. One approach to Snowdon includes a daunting walk along a sharp ridge or arête via the adjoining peak of Crib Goch. Often called the "Snowdon horseshoe", this ridge and the summit of Crib Goch can be seen clearly towards the right of this photograph, dominating the view of Llyn Llydaw in the foreground. Below, Glaslyn lies under Snowdon's pyramidal peak.

Llyn Idwal *(above)*

Located in arguably the most dramatic cwm in North Wales, Llyn Idwal is cradled by the three craggy peaks of Glyder Fawr, Twll Du and Y Garn. This footbridge at the lake's edge looks towards Y Gribin, a ridge extending from between the Glyders. Cwm Idwal is a nature reserve and the shallow cirque lake has unusually rich plant life and plenty of fish. It is also rich in legend. A moraine on the lake's western shore is said to be the burial place of the giant, Idwal. It is also said that no bird flies over the lake's surface, and that a wailing voice can be heard when there is a storm in the cwm.

Cwm Idwal with Tryfan and Glyders behind *(left)*

Cwm Idwal is also the most accessible cwm in Britain, just a short distance from one of the busiest roads in Wales. The nature reserve was the first to be established in Wales in 1954, and uses enclosures to explore the effect of sheep and goats grazing on the rich plant life. Heather and purple moor grass grows at the northern end of the lake, while at the southern end, where the lake becomes a stream with small waterfalls, sub-Arctic flora grows alongside tufted hair grass and yarrow. The cwm has attracted botanists, anglers, geologists and climbers for many years.

Llyn Padarn & the Snowdon range *(above and left)*

These attractive photographs show Llyn Padarn's most spectacular view: looking towards the famous Llanberis Pass with the Snowdon range's northern flank majestic in the afternoon sunlight. The lake is two miles long and situated in a wide glacial valley. On the lake's southern shore is Llanberis, from where the Snowdon Mountain Railway carries tourists to its summit by a five-mile scenic route. The entire valley is strewn with boulders, while hillside oak woodland and the Dinorwic slate quarries overlook the lake.

During the industrial age, Llyn Padarn was a commercial waterway, transporting ore from the copper mines around Nant Peris to Cwm-y-glo. It was not until 1830 that a road was built by the mining companies, enabling them to transport ore from Pen-y-Pass to Caernarfon more effectively. Today the lake is a scenic spot, and the site of the Llyn Padarn Country Park. Boats are available for hire, and the lake is a popular spot for canoeing, windsurfing and sailing. It is also popular with anglers and boasts excellent brown trout fishing.

Moelwyn Mawr *(above)*

The slopes of Moelwyn Mawr, viewed here from the summit ridge of Cnicht, are criss-crossed with paths and scarred with evidence of northern Snowdonia's industrial heritage. Quarries and their disused tips line the sides of Cwm Croesor, where lakes and reservoirs provided water power and inclines were built to transport hard-won slate to market. From the summit of Moelwyn Mawr and Cnicht, on rain-free days, the panorama is superb with views to almost all the mountains of Snowdonia.

Llanberis Pass *(right)*

The Afon Nant Peris runs along the length of the rugged Llanberis Pass, beside the pass road built in the early 19th century by the local mining companies. Among scree and rocky debris, the stream grows bigger as it is joined by others that tumble from the lofty heights of the Glyders and the Snowdon range. Climbers flock to Pen-y-Pass, the highest starting point for hikes to the Snowdon horseshoe.

Pen Yr Ole Wen and Cwm Idwal *(above)*

Clouds cast shadows on the soft and marshy ground that walkers must cross to reach the summit ridge of Pen yr Ole Wen. This aspect from beside Cwm Idwal, 1,220ft (370m) above sea level, towards Pen yr Ole Wen and the southerly mountains of the Carneddau range, is dramatic and geologically ancient. Charles Darwin and Professor Adam Sedgwick (widely regarded as the father of modern geology) visited Cwm Idwal in 1831 and examined rocks for fossils. Sedgwick did not believe that glaciers had any effect in shaping the landscape and so both scientists failed to spot the generous glacial evidence. Darwin later wrote that a house burnt down by fire could not have told its story more plainly than Cwm Idwal, but Sedgwick continued to refute the theory until his death 42 years after their visit.

Pen Yr Ole Wen & Ogwen Cottage

The path to Cwm Idwal starts at Ogwen Cottage, beside Llyn Ogwen and close to waterfalls on the Afon Ogwen. The scene is overlooked by the dark brow of Pen yr Ole Wen, a major mountain at the foot of the Carneddau range. Its steadily rising slope and crag-free south face makes it difficult to judge its enormous size, over 200ft (60m) higher than Tryfan across the pass. It is a relentless climb to the summit, with much scrambling across rock, but splendid panoramic views include breathtaking sights of the Menai Strait, Anglesey, Snowdon, the Glyders, Tryfan and the Carneddau.

Disused quarry below Foel Ddu

Slate-quarrying remains line the flanks of Cwm Croesor, just two miles from the slate capital of North Wales, Blaenau Ffestiniog. The Rhosydd Slate Quarry, under the shadow of Foel Ddu, quarried an estimated 220 million slates in its 80 year history. In one of the wettest parts of North Wales, slateworkers toiled both above and below ground, quarrying deeper with the years. At its peak in the 1880s, 200 workers mined 6,000 tons of saleable slate each year. Quarrymen would hike to barracks each Monday morning with enough food for the week. Rhosydd was notorious for its crowded and damp barracks and the worst living conditions in the industry. The evocative remains of the quarrymen's barracks still stand, although the mills were demolished in the 1940s for the slate in their walls. Underground mining took place in candlelight and eventually reached a depth of 14 floors, most of which are now flooded. In the early days, slate was transported to the Afon Dwyryd near Maentwrog by packhorse, but in 1864 a link was made to the Croesor Tramway, leading directly to Porthmadog.

Cnicht summit looking west to the Snowdon range

Majestic views of Snowdon and Crib Goch, beyond the fine valley of Nantgwynant, can be seen from the sharp and rocky summit of Cnicht. At 2,260ft (689m), the climb from Croesor is deceptively easy to start with and ends in a scramble, dangerous in this often wet and windy landscape. Views to the right of the Snowdon range reveal the Glyders, and to the left, the Hebogs. From roads to the south-west of Cnicht, the mountain appears pyramidal and has been called the Welsh Matterhorn. In fact the summit is on a fine ridge, and the pointed peak is a cross section of the mountain. The mountain range on which Cnicht stands stretches to the east where it ends at Moel Siabod; both are sometimes referred to as "the book ends".

Cnicht (left)

Looking south-west along the ridge from the summit of Cnicht are wonderful views of the Glaslyn Estuary (Traeth Bach). Behind the estuary lie the rugged Rhinog mountains, dotted with lakes and woodland. To the west are grand views of Cardigan Bay and the Lleyn peninsula. From the summit of Cnicht, and of the Moelwyn mountains to the south, steam trains of the Ffestiniog Railway can be heard as they curve and wind their way along the Vale of Ffestiniog to Porthmadog.

Llyn Ogwen & Tryfan
(below)

The towering crags of Tryfan stand alongside Llyn Ogwen in this magnificent photograph of bare mountain scenery. Llyn Ogwen is almost 990ft (300m) above sea level and one of the shallowest lakes in the area – an average of just 6ft (1.8m) deep. And yet trout thrive in its light blue waters. Around the lake, along an old fisherman's path, are grand views of Tryfan's giant buttresses, including the Milestone Buttress, one of the earliest crags to attract climbers.

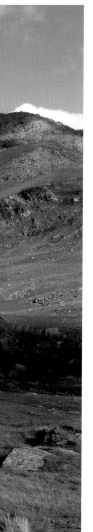

Llanberis and Snowdon

This idyllic late afternoon scene captures the true magic of Snowdonia in spring. Fine tufts of grass appear to flicker in the wind, beside heather and stray boulders patterned with lichen. Shadows on the sides of Snowdon add definition to the many ridges and valleys carved by glaciers in the Ice Age. Llanberis sits among thick forest at the foot of the mountain, beside a lake of striking blue. Mining is out of sight, but Llanberis developed entirely to support the industry, with slate mined at Dinorwic and copper mined on Snowdon's slopes. When mining came to an end, the village focused its energies on tourism. An ideal base for climbs to Snowdon's summit, both on foot and by train, the lake is also a magnet for anglers and watersports enthusiasts. The region's heritage is recorded in the Welsh Slate Museum.

Moel Siabod

The graceful peak of Moel Siabod (2861ft/872m) is the first mountain that many visitors will see as they enter Snowdonia National Park from Betws-y-Coed. At the foot of the mountain's eastern flanks lies Llyn y Foel. Behind it is the rough ridge that must be climbed to reach the top. From the rocky summit cairn are fine views over the sheer drop to Llynau Mymbyr and the cwm below. Under low and brooding clouds is a magnificent panorama, looking into the heart of Snowdonia, with the Snowdon horseshoe beautifully defined.

North-West Coast

The north-west coast of Wales takes in an array of scenic beauty including Anglesey and the thin finger of the Lleyn peninsula. Sandy bays and rocky coves line the cliff-backed coastlines. While the land is relatively low-lying, it is often backed dramatically by views of the Snowdonia mountains. Though remote, both the Lleyn peninsula and Anglesey are increasingly popular with holidaymakers seeking surf and sail. But history permeates at all levels, from the dramatic Victorian bridges that tower over the Menai Strait and spectacular Edwardian castles at Beaumaris, Conwy and Caernarfon, to stories of shipwrecks, Arthurian battles and the progress of Christian pilgrims. Colours are vivid, with green and fertile fields, brilliant blue bays, golden beaches and spectacular summer sunsets of all shades.

Menai Bridge

The Menai Suspension Bridge towers over the Menai Strait and separates the North Wales mainland from the Isle of Anglesey. Viewed from Church Island, the colours of the bridge and scenery are pronounced by the evening sunlight, while the foothills of Snowdonia are clearly visible. Designed by Thomas Telford and completed in 1826, a clearance of 100ft (30m) was required so that tall sailing ships could continue to travel along the Strait. The bridge was just one of many challenges Telford faced in improving the London to Holyhead route, essential for crossings to Ireland.

Conwy

The estuary at Conwy is dominated by Edward I's dark-stoned medieval castle and crossed by three parallel bridges. This photograph shows a clear view of Robert Stephenson's tubular railway bridge. Behind it are two further bridges for road traffic including a suspension bridge designed by Telford. The castle itself was constructed within four years and was a key fortress in Edward's fearsome "iron ring" of castles built to subdue the Welsh.

Benllech

The popular seaside resort of Benllech is famous for its fine golden sands and safe, blue waters which are ideal for paddling and bathing. Set in a crescent-shaped bay and surrounded by fossil-studded cliffs, the low tide reveals miles of beautiful beach. Walks from Benllech along the cliffs are ideal for nature-lovers, with birdwatching particularly good. The area is rich in ancient history: a neolithic burial chamber and the remains of 4th-century huts are close by, whilst the grave of a Viking was found in 1945 on a sandy ridge facing Benllech Sands.

Lavan Sands *(left)*

Coastal walks between Beaumaris and Penmon are largely determined by the tide. Picking your way along the foreshore among the rocks and seaweed gives views of the mainland across the Lavan Sands (Traeth Lafan). Before the Menai Suspension Bridge was built, ferries took passengers across the Strait here from Bangor to Beaumaris pier. The fast-moving tides often made this journey treacherous, and many boats capsized or ran aground.

Beaumaris pier *(right)*

The picturesque 13th-century town of Beaumaris is filled with brightly coloured antique shops and lively pubs, cafes and restaurants. The rambling mixture of medieval, Georgian, Victorian and Edwardian architecture gives Beaumaris a unique charm. There are breathtaking views of Snowdonia across the Menai Strait and plenty of opportunities for fishing and sailing on boats from the pier.

Until the 1950s, many thousands of tourists arrived in North Wales on paddle steamers from Liverpool. Some of the most popular routes stopped at Beaumaris pier on their way down the Menai Strait to Caernarfon. A landing stage and pavilion on the pier became unsafe after lack of maintenance and were demolished, but regular repair work has prevented any further deterioration.

Ynys Moelfre (right)

To the north of the town of Moelfre, across the narrow channel of Y Swnt, lies Ynys Moelfre, a small outcrop inhabited by seagulls and cormorants. In the distance are striking views of Snowdonia. These shallow waters have seen some of Moelfre's most challenging sea rescues including that of the Hindlea, a light coaster which, while at anchor, was dragged by hurricane force winds perilously close to the shore in October, 1959. The local lifeboat made 10 heroic journeys to the ship, managing to save all eight members on board.

Moelfre boathouse (far right)

This view of Moelfre's boathouse and slipway shows a calm and quiet sea, but the Moelfre lifeboat crew have been involved in many heroic rescues in strong winds, earning scores of medals for bravery. A lifeboat station was established at Moelfre in 1830, whilst this boathouse and slipway were constructed in 1909. The history of Moelfre's lifeboats is recorded on the inner walls of the lifeboat house and in a local museum.

Penmon

The rocks of the Penmon peninsula, located at the eastern tip of Anglesey, have been quarried for centuries and used in the construction of roads and castles, including nearby Beaumaris Castle. This photograph shows limestone rubble revealed by a low tide, while Puffin Island lies across a deceptively calm stretch of water. The island became a religious settlement in the sixth century.

Cemlyn Bay, lifeboat memorial

On the headland, Trwyn Cemlyn, is a prominent memorial stone commemorating the launch of Anglesey's first lifeboat in 1828. The Reverend James Williams of Llanfair-yn-Nghornwy and his wife, Frances, founded the Anglesey Association for the Preservation of Life from Shipwrecks, following the sinking of a sailing ship and loss of all 140 on board. The RNLI took over the association's work in 1885 and still protects life at sea around Anglesey today.

Cemlyn Bay, cliff views *(below)*

On Anglesey's north coast lies Cemlyn Bay, a two-mile stretch of coastline owned by the National Trust. On calm days such as this, cliff views can stretch to the Isle of Man. A saltwater lagoon here is run as a wildlife sanctuary. Cut off from the sea by a storm-driven shingle spit, the site is a haven for waders and seabirds. Many maritime plants including sea-kale grow on the headlands.

The Skerries *(above)*

At sunset, views of The Skerries and its famous lighthouse can be spectacular. Two miles off Carmel Head, on the north-west coast of Anglesey, this group of treeless, jagged rocks was a sailing blackspot for hundreds of years. A light was proposed as early as 1658, and the lighthouse's construction in the early 18th century made the isolated outcrop home to brave lighthouse-keepers for over 270 years. The lighthouse is now fully automated and was recently restored.

Bull Bay *(right)*

The rugged, rocky cove of Bull Bay (Porth Llechog) is a quiet and pleasant spot overlooked by hotels and a golf course. The bay has some beautiful cliff walks and the area is popular with fishermen and yachtsmen, when weather and tide permit. The English name, Bull Bay, is thought to be derived from the name of a pool on the beach, "Pwll y Tarw" or the Bull's Pool.

Cemaes Bay, harbour *(above)*

The natural, sheltered harbour of Cemaes Bay has become a centre for maritime activities. Classed as an Area of Outstanding Beauty, many of the bay's cliffs and beaches are owned by the National Trust. Sunsets over the bay are superb, and the changing seas and skies are popular with artists. Cemaes looks north to the Irish Sea and is the most northerly village in Wales. Shipbuilding took place in Cemaes, which for many years was the principal port on the north coast for trade in coal and stone. Mining activities on Parys Mountain led to the extension of the harbour, and to the development of nearby Amlwch Port.

Anglesey sunset across Menai Strait

The currents of the Menai Strait rush rapidly over bedrock and boulders in many parts and travel slowly in others, depositing mud and sand to create a rich environment for over 1,000 species of marine plants and animals. This dramatic sunset at low tide casts a pearly glow on deceptively calm waters. Changing tides in the channel can cause the water to swirl in different directions.

Red Wharf Bay *(below)*

On the east coast, Red Wharf Bay or Traeth Coch is the largest beach on Anglesey at low tide, but at high tide it is a lengthy five-mile walk around its muddy saltmarsh shores and sand dunes. As well as several small rock pools, the bay attracts a large number of waterfowl and wading birds including curlew, oystercatchers, purple sandpipers and grey plover.

Caernarfon

Boats moor in Caernarfon harbour, overlooked by the grand presence of Caernarfon castle's polygonal towers and curtain walls. One of Edward I's many military strongholds, the castle was positioned on a peninsula at the foot of the Menai Strait where Norman and Roman fortifications had once stood. The castle's design was inspired by the Roman city of Constantinople and the Eagle Tower, seen to the left, was crowned with stone eagles as a symbol of imperial power. Edward's son was born in the castle and became the first English Prince of Wales in 1301. In the 20th century, both Edward VIII and Prince Charles became Princes of Wales in controversial investiture ceremonies held in the castle. Four thousand guests attended Prince Charles' investiture, and an audience of 500m watched the event on television.

Criccieth *(left)*

The castle at Criccieth stands high on an outcrop of green felsite rock. Reached by a steep climb, the castle was originally built by the Welsh but was ruined by fire after changing hands several times. It has now been restored and a museum on the site explains its history. Criccieth is known as "the pearl of Wales on the shore of Snowdonia" and is most famous for its associations with David Lloyd George, the Liberal statesman and prime minister who grew up nearby and addressed crowds at political meetings in Market Square. Criccieth's two beaches, with safe swimming and bathing, are often visited by porpoises.

Porth Ysgo *(above and right)*

Beyond Abersoch, the coastline scenery of Lleyn changes dramatically to an astonishing landscape of ancient, time-worn rocks and boulders. Just 10 minutes from the road, a walk passes through a valley of ferns and foxgloves, and past a series of small waterfalls, before climbing down wooden steps to a sheltered bay of black gabbro rocks revealed at low tide. Formed from molten magma trapped beneath the earth's surface, these distinctive boulders give Porth Ysgo its otherwordly feel and indeed the area is steeped in legend.

Porth Alwm *(below)*

Manganese was mined on the Lleyn peninsula for over a century and nuggets can be found among the distinctive blue-black rocks on the shoreline. Six mines operated intermittently throughout the Victorian age and the first half of the 20th century. At first, pack mules carried baskets of ore from the mines to the beach, where it was loaded onto small steamships bound for Ellesmere Port. Later, jetties were built and ore was transported from the mines by cable car or rail, parts of which could still be seen on the beaches long after the mines closed down.

Aberdaron *(above)*

The whitewashed cottages of Aberdaron cluster beside the wide sand and shingle bay. Pilgrims on their way to Bardsey Island (Ynys Enlli) would depart from this remote fishing village, stopping for food and shelter at the 14th century Y-Gegin Fawr ("the Old Kitchen"). Day visits to the island can still be arranged, setting sail from Aberdaron. The Church of St Hywyn, with twin naves, was built in the 12th century by Gruffydd ap Cynan, King of Gwynedd, and enlarged in 1417. The stone buildings replaced wooden structures, which had been used for worship since the fifth century. It is a sanctuary church where disputes can be settled on the stone chair of peace, and no fugitive can be ejected for 40 days and nights.

Beach huts, Abersoch

The annual regatta at Abersoch includes a best-dressed beach hut competition – a chance for the lucky few to show off their home from home. With so many first-class events taking place offshore, and fantastic views to boot, beach huts are hot property. A dilapidated beach hut of just 12ft by 12ft recently sold for £39,500, a figure double the annual wage of most local people. Beach towns on Lleyn are among the most fashionable in Britain.

Aberdaron beach *(above and below)*

The beach can be busy in the summer months with surfing and sailing enthusiasts making their own pilgrimage to the wide bay. Offshore fishing trips can be organised, with beach fishing popular as well. Annual events, including a regatta with races for all levels and a festival with competitions and concerts bring hundreds of visitors to Aberdaron. Divers can explore an offshore wreck, known as *The Priscilla*, which sank in the 19th century. Much of the surrounding land is owned by the National Trust, and there are some fine coastal and clifftop walks that thread through gorse and follow in the footsteps of the medieval pilgrims, with superb views of Bardsey Island and the green fields of Lleyn.

Abersoch beaches

Horse-riding along the beach is just one of many ways to enjoy outdoor pursuits in Abersoch. Almost too successful, the town is hugely crowded at peak season and its three beaches are full of activity. The northernmost beach, known as The Warren, or Quarry beach, has good sand at low tide that stretches to the rocky headland of Trwyn Llanbedrog. Cliffs here reach up towards the mountain, Mynydd Tir-y-Cwmwd, which at 433ft (132m) has wonderful panoramic views that take in the great expanse of Cardigan Bay. Footpaths zigzag the headland, which is topped by a tin man sculpture that can be seen from the beach at Llanbedrog.

Uwchmynydd and Bardsey Island

The headland at the end of the Lleyn peninsula, generally referred to as Uwchmynydd, is the Land's End of North Wales. To get there, walkers pass over open grassland criss-crossed with sheep tracks and scattered with small fields, sheep and heather. The headland's summit, Mynydd Mawr, is a wild spot with magnificent views across the Bardsey Sound, a two-mile wide stretch of water with dangerous tides and currents, to Bardsey Island. So many Christian pilgrims sought sanctuary and were buried on the island that it became known as the Isle of 20,000 Saints and remains of graves can be seen across the island. Dominated by a hill over 500ft (152m) high, Enlli is a now a seabird sanctuary and wildlife refuge with many grey seals to be spotted along the shoreline.

Lleyn peninsula at sunset

During the daytime, the coast around the Lleyn peninsula is surrounded by golden, sandy coves and vibrant blue waters. The hills are covered with a patchwork of bright green fields and hedgerows. These colours are often transformed as the sun sets to giant red and orange streaked skies above the silvery seas and black silhouettes of headlands and clifftops. The magnificent pinks, yellows and blues in this scene are a reminder of the tranquillity and timelessness of the peninsula. Pilgrims walked for miles under sunsets such as these to reach Bardsey Island, and the sound of waves lapping at the shores and the barks of seals have been heard for centuries.

Porth Dinllaen and Carreg Ddu

The natural harbour of Porth Dinllaen was almost chosen for development as the main port for ferries to Ireland, but instead this role fell to Holyhead. The long, curving bay is backed by low cliffs. To the western end are clustered fishing cottages of the tiny 18th-century Porth Dinllaen hamlet now owned by the National Trust. The beach is perfect for picnics, walks and bathing and the red-painted Ty Coch Inn is an ideal place to stop for a bite to eat and a drink. From the promontory at Carreg Ddu are stunning views of the sweeping bay and the mountains of Snowdonia beyond. Seals can often be seen sunning themselves on the rocks here.

South and West Snowdonia

Southern Snowdonia may not have the drama of the high peaks of the Snowdon range but it is packed with mountain scenery and beautiful green valleys. Hikes in this region are refreshingly free of the crowds that flock further north, and begin in remote and secret valleys. The highest peaks in this region, Aran Fawddwy and Penygadair on Cadair Idris, are close to 3,000ft (915m) and steeped in the legend of giants. Views from the Cadair Idris range in particular extend as far as the Lleyn peninsula, with a fine outlook on the picturesque Mawddach estuary. The lakes here are mystical places with glassy blue waters and abundant wildlife. Popular with anglers, they are well-stocked with wild brown and rainbow trout.

Penygadair (right)

Cyfrwy (the Saddle) reaches 2,660ft (811m) and is the third highest summit along the Cadair Idris ridge with dramatic cliffs. When the Victorians discovered the Welsh mountains, Cadair Idris became a popular climb for many tourists on hired ponies with guides. An old lady trekked early each morning to the Penygadair summit hut to serve many grateful visitors cups of tea.

Cadair Idris (above)

It is just a short scramble among the loose stones south of Penygadair to this wonderful viewpoint. It is reached by the Minfford Path, a route to three peaks that requires energy and fitness and is exceedingly steep in places. The route follows the rim around Craig Cau with sheer drops towards Llyn Cau with its deep green-blue waters and glasslike appearance. Looking south, the slope down to the valley at Talyllyn is extremely long. This ridge is one side of the 20km (12 mile) Bala-Talyllyn fault, the largest land shift in Wales. The classic U-shaped valley here was carved by glaciers that exploited the natural weakness of the fault. Beyond the rift valley of Talyllyn lie the green humps of Plynlimon mountain.

Aran Fawddwy

It is a dramatic 1,000ft (305m) drop from the summit of Aran Fawddwy to the lake of Creiglyn Dyfi below. Seen here from Drws Bach, this solitary lake nestles below the towering crags of the ridge. No more than 600ft (183m) across, it is the source of the Afon Dyfi, which flows through Machynlleth to the sea at Aberdyfi and forms a natural boundary between north and south Wales. The river meets Bwlch y Groes (Pass of the Cross), the highest road in North Wales. Passing through a wild and barren landscape travellers discovered a cross at its highest point – a chance to "thank God" for having completed the climb. Today a wooden cross stands where the road meets the turning point for Lake Vyrnwy (Llyn Efyrnwy).

Aran Fawddwy, the summit cairn

The stony summit cairn of Aran Fawddwy is said to have been erected by the men of Dinas Mawddwy when they believed Cadair Idris to be 6ft (2m) higher. In fact Aran Fawddwy was found to be 43ft (13m) higher than Penygadair. Both Aran Fawddwy and Aran Benllyn, a mile along the ridge, are associated with Arthurian legends. King Arthur is said to have fought a mighty battle nearby with a giant, Rhita Gawr, who lived on the southern edge of Aran Fawddwy. The giant wished to make a collar for his robe from Arthur's beard. Arthur fought the giant and won, flinging him down the hillside. Aran Benllyn is one of the many places the giant is said to have been buried.

25

Aran Fawddwy summit

To reach the summit of Aran Fawddwy it is a
steady climb from the head of a lovely and secret
valley. Crowning the highest ridge of southern
Snowdonia, the mountain summit is higher than
Cadair Idris at 2,976ft (905m). This rewarding view
from the rocky plateau takes in the sister peak of
Aran Benllyn and to the right, Cwm Croes. Beyond
and out of view in this photograph lies Bala Lake
(Llyn Tegid), a base for many who hike and climb
in the Arans.

Cwm Cywarch *(right and far right)*

It is likely that hemp was cultivated in Cwm
Cywarch, as the name translates as Hemp Valley.
Widely grown across Britain during the Middle
Ages, hemp was used for textiles, paper, rope and
oil production. Farmers were required to grow
hemp to supply the navy with fibres for ropes and,
in the 1800s, Harlech was a centre for hemp
production. Yellow Welsh poppies grow in the
peaceful valley and the tussocky landscape is dotted
with trees and a number of small farmsteads. The
rocky crags of Cwm Cywarch are a magnet for
climbers and there are opportunities for birdwatching with buzzards often seen circling high
above the cliffs.

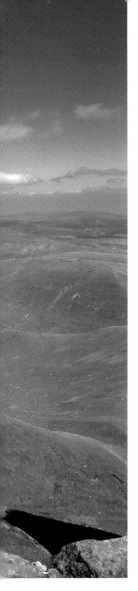

Cadair Idris summit *(above)*

Cadair Idris means the chair of Idris, who may have been Idris Gawr, a Celtic poet and giant of legend who liked to study the stars from his high throne. In one popular story, though it is not a tale exclusive to Cadair Idris, a visitor who spends a night alone on the summit of the mountain will return either as a madman or a poet.

Memorial cairn, Drws Bach

The Aran ridge begins at Drws Bach, which translates as the "little door" and stands at 2,500ft (762m). Hikes from Cwm Cywarch that climb the side of Cwm Hengwm reach the ridge through this narrow doorway. A memorial cairn stands here, built to honour SAC Michael Robert Aspin of RAF Mountain Rescue, killed by lightning in 1960. Views from the cairn are outstanding, with sharp drops into Cwm Hengwm in front, and a shallower descent behind, with marvellous views of Creiglyn Dyfi and Aran Fawddwy's eastern face.

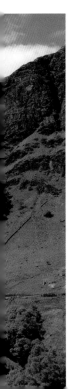

Llynnau Cregennen

The crystal clear blue waters of the Llynnau Cregennen are edged by grassy reeds and small boulders. These two magical lakes lie 750ft (230m) above the Mawddach Estuary in a green and undulating plateau landscape surrounded by heather-clad mountains. The craggy face of Tyrrau Mawr looms imposingly above the waters, and the heights of Cadair Idris lie further beyond. At several points close to the lakes, and especially from the peak of Tyrrau Mawr, there are magnificent views of the Afon Mawddach, Barmouth and the remote Lleyn peninsula. The lakes are stocked with wild brown and rainbow trout, and the serene atmosphere makes this an ideal place to spend a day fishing.

Once privately owned, the lakes were given to the National Trust in 1959 by Major CL Wynne-Jones in memory of his two sons who were both killed in the Second World War. Several groups of prehistoric standing stones can be found among the fields of sheep and in the forest, many in spectacular settings. The stones are thought to be close to a Bronze Age trackway known as Fford Ddu (The Dark Road) whose route from Tywyn eventually found its way to the Cotswolds.

Llangollen *(left)*

The picturesque scenery of the River Dee (Afon Dyfrdwy) is seen here from Llangollen's famous and elegant bridge. The town's centrepiece, the bridge was built by Bishop Trevor in 1345 and today carries motor traffic and, during the summer, international visitors and musicians at Llangollen's lively annual International Eisteddfod. Surrounded by hills, and overlooked by the ruins of the 13th-century Castell Dinas Bran, Llangollen is an ideal place for a leisurely and historic walk. Weirs, falls and miniature rapids can all be found along the river, alongside which runs Thomas Telford's historic road from London to Holyhead and the scenic Llangollen Railway. The fine ruins of a 13th-century Cistercian monastery, Valle Crucis Abbey, are also found close by.

Llyn Trawsfynydd *(below)*

In this, one of the strongholds of the Welsh language, lies the calm lake of Trawsfynydd surrounded by nature trails. Boats can be hired for a day's leisurely fishing – the lake is popular with the angling community and well-stocked with wild brown and rainbow trout. For 28 years Llyn Trawsfynydd supplied the waters for an atomic power station here. The station closed in 1993, but a visitor centre explains how electricity was generated.

Llyn Cynwch *(above)*

Near Llanfachreth and the village of Nannau lies Llyn Cynwch, a favourite location for anglers, since the lake is stocked with trout regularly throughout the fishing season. A long and narrow sheet of water, the lake is tucked away amongst wooded hillsides of larch and oak. Cadair Idris provides a fine background at its southern end. Parts of the well-known Precipice Walk skirt the side of the lake. The walk follows a gentle route around the low hill of Moel Cynwch and leads to a precipice with outstanding views high above the Mawddach Estuary – across to Barmouth and the sea, as well as south to the Cadair Idris massif.

Evening sun, Moel-y-Gest *(above)*

The climb to the summit of Moel-y-Gest, just 859ft (262m) above the town of Porthmadog, is not too strenuous and passes the remains of a granite quarry. Though the quarry was closed in the 1920s, the incline used to transport the granite can still be seen. From the top are spectacular views of the surrounding hills and mountains, including Moel Ddu and Moel Hebog seen in the evening sun in this spectacular photograph. The green valley below is scattered with cottages for rent where walkers can enjoy a picturesque and restful base for travels into nearby Snowdonia.

Afon Glaslyn estuary *(below)*

Half a mile from Borth-y-Gest, it is an easy climb to the summit of Moel-y-Gest, from which there are spectacular views across Traeth Bach to Harlech and the Rhinog mountains beyond. It is said that Prince Madog, the son of Owain Gwynedd, set sail from Borth-y-Gest to discover America, 300 years before Christopher Columbus. At low tide, the course of the Afon Glaslyn can be seen, as well as the mainly agricultural land reclaimed from the saltmarsh and mudflats of the estuary. The sands of Traeth Bach are unsafe for bathing because of strong currents and fast incoming tides.

Quayside, Porthmadog *(above)*

Slate from the mines of Snowdonia was shipped from Porthmadog harbour to destinations such as Hamburg, Cadiz and South America. Porthmadog went into decline in the 1870s with the arrival of the Cambrian railway and the decline of the slate trade and today the town has become a centre for tourism. The old slate sheds that lined the quayside have been replaced with holiday flats, seen here beneath the Rhinog mountains beyond.

Mudflats, Glaslyn estuary *(below)*

From the south side of the Cob, the wide mudflats of the Glaslyn Estuary are revealed at low tide. Before the causeway was built, the estuary was said to be the most beautiful in the whole of Wales. Today, it is a haven for migrating birds and wildlife, and can hold up to 1,500 wigeon in the winter as well as smaller numbers of waders and wildfowl such as Canada geese, mallard and teal. Several beaches around the headland have fine golden sands and small coves.

Harlech Castle, early evening

Built by Edward I in the late 13th century, the commanding castle
at Harlech almost grows from the rock on which it stands. Once,
the waters of Tremadog Bay lapped the foot of the castle; today
the castle, a World Heritage Site, looks over extensive sand dunes
that back the wide golden sands of Harlech Beach.

Mawddach Estuary from Precipice Walk

A circular two-mile route known as the Precipice Walk has superb
views of the Mawddach Estuary and Llyn Cynwch, as well as
views south to Cadair Idris. The estuary runs nine miles inland to
Dolgellau and its beauty has been the inspiration for many artists
and writers. Turner painted scenes here and Wordsworth described
the estuary as "sublime" and comparable to the finest in Scotland.
Much of Charles Darwin's *The Descent of Man* was written in a
house overlooking the estuary, whilst John Ruskin said that the
only journey in the world that had views to compare with the one
from Dolgellau to Barmouth, was the journey from Barmouth to
Dolgellau.

First published in 2009 by Myriad Books Limited,
35 Bishopsthorpe Road London SE26 4PA

Photographs copyright © Simon Kirwan
Text copyright © Hilary Ellis

ISBN 1 84746 244 8
EAN 978 1 84746 244 2

Designed by Jerry Goldie Graphic Design Printed in China

www.myriadbooks.com

Front cover: Penygadair; back cover: Moel Siabod; title page: Gallt-yr-ogof and Tryfan